" Reflections ...
    for touching hearts "

... all thoughts are originals of :~

--- Brock Tully

illustrations :~

--- Heidi Thompson

calligraphy :~

--- Brock Tully

~other books by Brock Tully~
1. Reflections~for someone special
2. Reflections~for living life fully
3. Reflections~for sharing dreams
4. Coming Together~ a 10,000 mile
                    bicycle journey.
    5. With Hope We Can All Find
        Ogo Pogo~for the child in us all.

*Heidi Thompson~ 9905 Cold Stream Creek Rd. Vernon, B.C., Canada, V1B 1C8 ~ (604) 542-1551

Dedication...

... to all those store owners who've lent me a pen & scrap piece of paper, when i was out jogging, & a little thought came 'popping out' of my heart. ☺

... i first started writing little thoughts
as a way of listening to, ¦ becoming closer
to my heart ...

"... when i love
                'to grow',
        i seem to
                grow more loving."

... my constant challenge is 'to live' the
thoughts i write so that my actions will be
a reflection of my heart ...

"... to grow, at first,
        seemed like slow, hard work,
    but my life is becoming
                easier ¦ easier...
    When i looked for the quick
            ¦ easy way out,
        my life became
                harder."

"... without even touching me,
        you touch me,
    by massaging
            my heart
        with your presence."

"... being special
               isn't necessarily
           doing things differently...

       it's finding it necessary
               that the things we do
       make a difference."

"... i used to believe
        what others believed
                        i should do ---

now that i'm 'believing in' me,
    i find others
            are leaving me 'be'."

"... if you're not happy with me
& i change for you,
it likely won't last long ...
... if i change
for me,
i'll like who i am,
& i'll be happy
at long last."

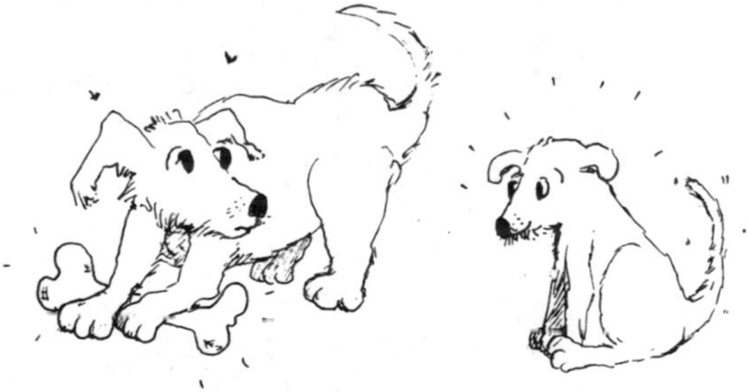

"... often,
　　with choices,
　the hard part isn't
　　'knowing'
　　What we should do ...

but,
　　'doing'
　　　What we know
　　We should do."

"... when i base how well
                    i know people
           by how long
                    i've known them,
often,
     in a moment,
          my heart is hurt
     When i find i never really knew them
                         at all ...

When my heart is open to people
               the moment i meet them,
     sometimes,
          i feel like i've known them
                    for a long time,
          & my heart would have been hurt most
               if i hadn't been open."

"... since i've stopped
                going back
          to what i need
                to leave behind ...
i've started
                looking forward
          to what
                lies ahead."

"... i think it's alright
                    to be sure...
but not to be
                    'so sure'
        that i think
            i have to
        always be right."

" ... my reliability
should never depend on
Who i know better ...
it's knowing
i better be dependable
With Whoever."

"... i now know
            that trust
    isn't based on
            the length of time
    i've known someone...
but,
    how i'm feeling
                with someone
    at that moment
                in time."

"... i'd rather die,
                 living,
    than to die
        slowly,
                  not living...
    & since i've started
                  living,
        i'm less afraid
                of dying,
        except from the death
        of not living."

"---at this moment...

i hope
you are feeling
as wonderful
as i
feel you 'are'---

--- at every moment."

" happiness, for me,
    isn't being
        all smiles ...

happiness
    is being able
        to smile,
    knowing i am,
        however i feel
    like being."

" ... too often
        committments mean
                a loss of freedom
                & becoming a follower ...
    by becoming committed
                to following my heart,
        i've become freer."

"... sometimes
        i say i don't like
                the way some people are...
because at times
        i am the way
                i don't like others
                        to be."

" --- a strength
          isn't 'acting' real strong ---
a strength
          is to quit acting
                    & be real."

"--- When we're babies,
    We just 'are',
        & we don't worry about
    What we're going 'to be'---
When we grow up,
    We worry about
            What we're going 'to be',
    & we often stop being who we 'are'."

"... i used to waste time
                    worrying
            about what others thought ---
now i think about
            what a waste of time
      it is to worry."

"... i always love
            to see you...
but,
    i don't have
            to see you,
    to always
            love you."

"... the more i look
        for the perfect person
                to fulfill me,
        the more possessive i am
                for fear of losing them...
the more that i see
        that we are all perfect,
        ¿ it's the journey
of staying in touch
                with that perfection
        that's so fulfilling,
the more i allow
                others to grow,
        ¿ i become closer to them."

"... i used to look for ways
                to get high
    so i'd enjoy
                living more ---

    now,
        i get high more,
            but it's from
        'the joy of living.'"

"... enough times i've said
      'i'm only one person,
   What can i do?'...
now,
    i only want to say
          'i'm one person
    who can never do enough !"

"... building walls around me
                    takes energy,
   & i feel old & tired ..."

When i tire of building walls
              i have lots of energy,
   & i feel young again!"

"...growth lies
        in truth...
    not in
            lies."

"... before,
    i met people
    hoping to find
            the love i needed ...
now,
    i find my needs
            are met,
    just by being
        a "loving being.""

"... i may not
        always believe
    what you
            say & do...

    but,
        i can always say
            i do
        'believe in' you."

"... the sad part
       of a tragedy
   is the loss
       of a beautiful person
           we were close to...
the tragic part
       of this sadness
is if we don't see
       that it's through this loss
that we can gain
       so much closeness
           with ourselves & others."

"... i used to feel spent
        wondering
            what you were feeling...
now,
    it's a wonderful feeling
                spending time with you,
        knowing we can share
            'whatever' we are feeling."

"... since i've stopped
'needing'
to see you ...

i've started liking
what i've needed
to see 'in' me."

"... i was told
            i'd be
    'out-of-my-mind'
            to go after my dreams ...
now that i've gotten
    out of my mind
            by following my heart ...

    ... i'm living my dreams!"

"... i want you
              to love me,
  & i want you
              to need my love,
but,
    i don't want you
              to need me ...

... unless you want
              to knead me
    like 'a piece of bread'! ☺

"... the most unselfish thing
                    i can do
         is to be selfish
                    about doing
                    what makes me happy...

     it's when i'm happiest
            that i give most
                    to others."

"... when i'm happy
              in a relationship with someone,
     i love the way
                    they are ---

in a frustrating relationship with someone,
                   i'm unhappy with
     the way they are,
                ¿ i'm in love with
     the way
              i think they can be."

" ... you feel
   'beautiful'
  when you
      "be u to the fullest."

"... When i compete ...
it's not so important
that i be
better than,
but that i do
the best i can."

"--- We can try
to stand out in life,
by looking as good
as we can ---

or,

We can have
an outstanding life,
by looking for the good,
as we all can."

"... i feel i'm quitting
        when i 'stay' at something
                        i don't like ...
    because i've quit looking
                        for what
            i'd like to do
                    the most."

"... it hurts that others
            want to hurt us ...
    it hurts more,
            if we don't see
        that others want to hurt us
            because they've been hurt
                        by others...
    ; it hurts most,
            if we want to hurt others
                    because others
        have wanted to hurt us."

* as Gandhi said so beautifully...
        ... 'an eye for an eye
            ; we'll all be blind.'

" ... When i say
            beautiful things,
    i'm not necessarily
                    living them ...
When i live them,
        the beautiful thing
    is that words
                aren't necessary. "

"... the unconditional love
            you have shown me
        in a moment,
    has shown me,
            that it 'is' possible
                    to love,
            at every moment,
    under all conditions."

"... my greatest fear
        is that i become afraid,
because i listen
                to what others think
        i should be
                afraid of."

"... the love
            of power,
      is unloving ...
Whereas,
      'to love'
      is empowering."

"... i'd rather
          make mistakes,
   & find out
             who i am ---

than make the mistake
       of being afraid,
   & always wonder
             'who am i'?"

"... i'm sharing these thoughts,
not to be 'right'...
but because i believe
it's right
for me to share."

'a list of special movies'

"Gandhi"   ~ "Running Brave"
"Mask"   ~ "Silkwood"
"Dead Poet's Society"   ~ "Elephant Man"
"The Color Purple"   ~ "Harold & Maude"
"Ordinary People"   ~ "Jesus Christ Superstar"
"Cry Freedom"   ~ "Wings of Desire"
"Field of Dreams"   ~ "Children of a Lesser God"
"E.T."   ~ "Shirley Valentine"

* see first 2 Reflection books
    for lists of special books.

* by the way, Jon-Lee Kootnekoff
    has finally written a special book...
        "From Kooty,
                With Love"

... distributed by Simon & Schuster
(Green Tiger Division)
1 (800) 223-2348 (U.S.)
General Publishing
(416) 445-3333 (Canada)

* printed on recycled paper.